ESSENTIAL 100

GROUP STUDY GUIDE

Your journey through the Bible
in 100 readings

Written by Andy Twilley
© Scripture Union
First published 2011, reprinted 2017
ISBN 978 1 84427 585 4

Scripture Union
Trinity House, Opal Court, Opal Drive, Fox Milne, Milton Keynes, MK15 0DF, England
Email: info@scriptureunion.org.uk
Website: www.scriptureunion.org.uk

Scripture quotations are taken from the HOLY BIBLE, NEW INTERNATIONAL VERSION. Copyright © 1973, 1978, 1984 by International Bible Society. Anglicisation copyright © 1979, 1984, 1989, 1995, 1996, 2001. Used by permission of Hodder & Stoughton Ltd.

British Library Cataloguing-in-Publication Data
A catalogue record for this book is available from the British Library.

Printed in Malta by Gutenberg Press Ltd.
Cover design, internal design and typesetting by Heather Knight.

Scripture Union is an international Christian charity working with churches in more than 130 countries.

Thank you for purchasing this book. Any profits from this book support SU in England and Wales to bring the good news of Jesus Christ to children, young people and families and to enable them to meet God through the Bible and prayer.

Find out more about our work and how you can get involved at:
www.scriptureunion.org.uk (England and Wales)
www.suscotland.org.uk (Scotland)
www.suni.co.uk (Northern Ireland)
www.scriptureunion.org (USA)
www.su.org.au (Australia)

CONTENTS

THE E100 CHALLENGE

The E100 programme is being used all over the world, challenging people to make a commitment to reading the Bible. The Challenge is based around 100 carefully selected readings (50 from the Old Testament and 50 from the New Testament) and is designed to give participants a good understanding of the overall Bible story from Genesis to Revelation. The programme is very flexible and can be used by individuals or groups in the context of the local church.

We hope that completing the E100 Challenge will encourage you to continue spending regular time with God through Bible reading and prayer.

Essential 100 (written by Whitney T Kuniholm) is a key resource for this journey of discovery. For further information and additional materials – including sermon outlines and publicity resources – go to: www.e100challenge.org.uk.

INTRODUCING...

Essential 100: Group Study Guide

These small group studies are designed to complement *Essential 100*. There are 20 study outlines based around the 20 sections of 5 readings that make up the E100 programme. It is recommended that all study group members follow the E100 readings plan while your group is using this group study guide.

The studies aim to help your small group talk about topics and issues raised during each set of the five days' readings in *Essential 100*. They will provide an opportunity to share what God has said to you through the preceding week's readings, including questions or difficulties that have been encountered in the Bible passages. Your group discussions will work best if each member has already read most or all of the five readings.

This resource aims to help your group:

- Explore further the E100 Bible passages.
- Share questions and insights.
- Encourage one another in your journey through the Bible.
- Hear from God together and grow in your relationship with him.

We hope you will be encouraged on your journey through the E100 Challenge as you use these small group studies with others.

Each study includes...

This week's readings

The five readings for the week – you'll find the devotional note for each day's reading in *Essential 100*.

THE BIG STORY

This occasional section includes some of the key points in the big Bible story to look out for in the week's readings.

Way in

This aims to help the group start thinking about the week's topic and could be linked into a short time of worship.

Review

A look back at the week's readings. Encourage the group to give feedback on what they have read, inviting people to share what they have written on the 'review' page of *Essential 100*. Ask open questions such as:

What has excited you?
What has puzzled you?
What has challenged you?

This section also provides a brief summary of the five readings as a reminder and background for 'Going deeper'.

Going deeper

This is the heart of the session, when you're aiming to get to grips with the material. Insights from all group members should be encouraged, with an emphasis on the practical outworking of the Bible passages in our daily lives.

There will inevitably be differences of opinion sometimes. Handle such times with sensitivity. Occasionally you may simply need to agree to disagree!

Some topics will be very personal to members of your group. Always be ready to break away from your prepared study if it becomes apparent that someone in the group needs to be helped or comforted in some way.

Respond

This personal application is a key time as you allow the Holy Spirit to challenge you and use the Bible to change lives.

Encourage group members to think about:

What has this said to me?
What difference is it going to make to my view of God? To my daily life?

Sometimes there is an optional suggestion for an activity or object to act as a focus for this section. You may need to make some small preparation in advance for this.

DEVELOPING A SUCCESSFUL GROUP

Good preparation

Think and pray about each part of the study before you meet. Ask the Holy Spirit to guide you – whether you are a group participant or leading the session. Particularly, ask for God's help in dealing with issues that arise in your discussion that you had not anticipated.

Other resources

Draw on other resources to complement the material in this book. You may find it helpful to look at the introductory sections in *Essential 100* before each section of readings, or to look up relevant sections in commentaries or other Bible resource books like *Explorer's Guide to the Bible* (John Grayston, Scripture Union).

Variety

Use different approaches to stimulate discussion and raise issues. Resource books such as *Multi-Sensory Worship* and *Multi-Sensory Scripture* (Sue Wallace, Scripture Union) will provide a host of ideas.

Sensitivity

Be sensitive to the needs of each person in the group – and to issues that might upset individuals because of personal situations.

Some will need encouragement to share their thoughts and insights, whereas others may need holding back!

Support

Try to create an atmosphere in which everyone present feels relaxed and able to share at whatever level they are comfortable to do so. These group studies aim to provide mutual encouragement to continue on your journey through *Essential 100* – and the Bible.

1   In the beginning

This week's readings...

Genesis 1,2
Genesis 3
Genesis 6:5 – 7:24
Genesis 8:1 – 9:17
Genesis 11:1–9

Essential 100 pages 13–19

THE BIG STORY

The fall of human beings leads to the first of God's promises to man: a descendant of the woman will redeem fallen man... so the story of the Messiah begins.

After the Flood, God makes his first covenant with mankind. Look out for the rainbow – the special sign to Noah of God's promise.

Way in

Encourage each group member to say what element of creation they appreciate most and why. Use this as the basis for worship and praise to God for the wonder of his creation.

Review

Encourage the group to give feedback on this week's readings, inviting people to share what they have written on the 'review' page of *Essential 100*.

- God was from the very beginning. He created human beings and gave them two distinctives: God's life and God's standards.

- The first sin was about the questioning and challenging of God's will, followed by disobedience, resulting in the breakdown of a relationship with God.

- God is not watching and waiting to catch people out, as if it gives him pleasure to punish. Rather, sin causes God pain and grief.

- Noah's first response on leaving the ark was to worship God.

- The sin surrounding the building of the Tower of Babel was not about the technological achievement it represented, but the pride that went with it.

Going deeper

Creation

What do you think are the important issues surrounding the Bible's account of creation? How can the biblical view of creation be reconciled with our scientific knowledge? (Be careful that the issue of creation versus evolution doesn't take over the whole of your time! Christians have different views on this topic and it's important, of course, to listen to one another with respect and in love!)

What impact does 'God as creator' have on your view of him?

Sin

The heart of sin is rebellion against God, resulting in a breakdown of our relationship with him.

Some sins are sins of commission – doing things that are wrong; some are sins of omission – where we fail to do something we know we should (James 4:17). Talk about some specific examples of both from your experience. Do you tend to focus on one category or another?

Read Galatians 5:19–21 and Matthew 25:41–46, and then discuss the challenges these passages raise.

Worship

When we experience something really good in our lives, what is our first response? Do we simply enjoy it, or do we first express our appreciation to God? In practical terms, what should we learn from the account of how Noah responds to God after leaving the ark?

Respond

Give everyone a cut-out heart shape. Write on your 'heart' any issues from the areas above that you know you struggle with. Are you doing something you know is wrong? Or can you identify an attitude that is not really what God would want?

Spend a few minutes in silence praying about the things that are challenging you at the moment, asking that God will help you change where it matters.

If appropriate for your group, allow time to pray for each other.

Remembering Noah's response of worship, spend a few minutes thanking and worshipping God for his faithfulness to you and for what he's done for you.

2   Abraham, Isaac and Jacob

This week's readings...

Genesis 12
Genesis 15
Genesis 21:1 – 22:19
Genesis 27,28
Genesis 32,33

Essential 100 pages 20–26

THE BIG STORY

Abraham (first called Abram) is chosen by God to become the father of his special people. God makes a covenant with Abram and promises to create a great nation from his descendants.

The ancestral line of the Messiah (Jesus) is traced through Abraham, Isaac, Jacob and Judah.

Way in

Ask everyone to talk about where they were born, and then about the different places they have lived over the years. Share the reasons why each move took place, and the significance for your lives of new homes, schools, jobs, friends, relatives, children etc.

Using a map, look at where Abram was born (the city of Ur) and show how he travelled from there to Canaan via Haran.

Review

Invite the group members to share what they have written on the 'review' page of *Essential 100*, and to give reactions to what they have read.

- Abram showed great faith by obeying God and setting out on the journey to Canaan.
- God promised that, despite Abram and Sarai's age, they would have a son and his descendants would become a great nation. God gave Abram a new name, 'Abraham', meaning 'father of many'.
- Abraham was ready to obey God's command to sacrifice his son.
- Jacob tricked his father, Isaac, and received the blessing that should have been Esau's. He fled, travelling north to Haran. On his journey, he had a special encounter with God.

▪ Jacob sought to be reconciled to his brother. Esau demonstrated great grace as he welcomed him back.

Going deeper

Failure

Failure does not result in God abandoning us. Talk about the ways in which both Abraham and Jacob fail.

What has caused the failures? What does God do in each circumstance? What can we learn from this when thinking about our own failures?

Guidance

Discerning God's direction is often very challenging for us. How should we handle times of not knowing the exact details of what God wants? Encourage everyone to share ways in which God has revealed his plans to them. Talk about biblical ways of hearing God speak today.

God's promise

Discuss the implications of God's promise in Genesis 28:14 and Jacob's profession of faith in 28:20–22. Look at Galatians 3:14 to help you think about the implications of these verses for Christians today.

Reconciliation

The idea of reconciliation is often much easier than the reality. What are the faults and good qualities shown by Jacob and Esau?

Read the parable of the unforgiving servant (Matthew 18:21–35) and Jesus' words in Matthew 6:14,15. What are the key principles we need to incorporate into our relationships?

Respond

Write the words 'Failure', 'Guidance', 'God's promise' and 'Reconciliation' on sheets of paper, enough for one each for everyone in the group.

Scatter these on the floor and ask everyone to pick up a sheet showing an issue about which they feel God has been speaking to them. As people feel able, share thoughts about the following:

What does God want to say to you?
What reassurance do you need from God?

If there someone with whom you have had a fundamental breakdown of relationship, what is God calling you to do to put things right?

Pray for each person in your group, asking that they would experience a sense of God's love, his direction for the future and his grace to bring reconciliation where it is needed.

3   The story of Joseph

This week's readings...

Genesis 37
Genesis 39–41
Genesis 42
Genesis 43,44
Genesis 45:1 – 46:7

Essential 100 pages 27–33

THE BIG STORY

God's people are saved from the famine through their move to Egypt. Around 400 years later, this will be the scene for God's rescue of his people from slavery in the Exodus.

Way in

Joseph and the Amazing Technicolor Dreamcoat has been a top West End musical for many years. Has anyone in your group seen or participated in it? Invite people to share when and where this was. Encourage them to talk about which parts they liked most. You may even want to suggest going as a group to see it.

Review

Invite the group members to share what they have written on the 'review' page of *Essential 100*, and to give reactions to what they have read.

- Joseph's dreams made his brothers very angry, resulting in their selling him into slavery in Egypt.
- Joseph resisted the tempting of Potiphar's wife. His resulting time in prison provided the opportunity for him to explain the dreams of other prisoners, and even of Pharaoh himself.
- The famine made it necessary for Joseph's brothers to go to Egypt to find food.
- Despite all that his brothers had done, Joseph still loved them dearly. A few tricks, however, were played before there was reconciliation.
- Joseph made himself known to his brothers.

Going deeper

When we go through difficult times or temptations, we can respond in a number of ways.

Place a large sheet of paper in the centre of your group and ask a volunteer to write down what you discover as you talk. Start by writing the following headings on your paper: 'Situations', 'Possible responses' and 'Joseph's positive responses'.

Work through the past week's Bible passages, identifying the range of situations Joseph is faced with that have the potential of a positive or negative response. With each, highlight the different emotions or responses he could experience (eg pride, arrogance, rejection, jealousy, resentment, anger).

Explore the positive ways in which Joseph responds, such as:

• ensuring the offences against him didn't lead to negative responses

• showing himself morally strong when tempted

• being willing to serve others

• trusting that ultimately God was in control.

How could we build similar response patterns into our lives?

Respond

This study could stir a range of painful emotions that God wants to deal with.

You may be feeling hurts from years ago, which have stayed unresolved or which have led to bitterness and resentment. Or, you may be going through times of isolation, be a victim of injustice or be feeling uncertain about how present difficulties can be resolved.

The Bible story you have been thinking about this week is an important reminder that even when everything seems to be falling apart around us, God still has a plan and he is in control.

Encourage people to express their hurts in ways that are appropriate for them, and then pray specifically for each other.

4   Moses and the Exodus

This week's readings...

Exodus 1,2
Exodus 3:1 – 4:17
Exodus 6:28 – 11:10
Exodus 12:1–42
Exodus 13:17 – 14:31

Essential 100 pages 34–40

THE BIG STORY

The Passover is a key symbol that speaks of the death of Jesus, the Lamb of God. Like a lamb, he was slaughtered to rescue God's people from death.

Way in

Get the group to come up with a list of biblical characters who, from a human point of view, were surprising choices for God to use (eg Gideon, David).

Who do you know or have known who has been used in significant ways by God, despite obvious shortcomings or difficulties.

Review

Invite the group members to share what they have written on the 'review' page of *Essential 100*, and to give reactions to what they have read.

- Moses was miraculously rescued by one of Pharaoh's daughters and was brought up in the Egyptian royal court. On an impulse, he attempted to set the Israelites free from slavery by force. This resulted in him having to flee the country.
- Years later, God spoke to Moses through the burning bush.
- A sequence of disasters hit Egypt, giving Pharaoh opportunities after each to allow the people of Israel to leave Egypt.
- A climax came with the celebration of the Passover supper.
- In an amazing demonstration of God's power, the Red Sea was parted and the Israelites crossed to the safety of the desert beyond.

Going deeper

Moses is an ordinary man with an extraordinary mission. Explore some of the following issues together:

Older people

Moses is 80 when God calls him to lead his people out of Egypt. God continues using people in their old age. What does this say to your church in a time when society seems to think that those over 50 have less to offer?

Trust and obedience

'Trust' and 'obey' are key words from these readings, with Moses' call to go to Pharaoh, the challenges of the signs before Pharaoh and, finally, the action required for the parting of the Red Sea.

What does this say to us, both for life in general and for those times when God specifically calls us to do something?

Passover

What are the implications of the Passover supper:

• in terms of judgement on Egypt?

• as a symbolic reminder for the Israelites for the years ahead?

• as a pointer to the life and death of Jesus?

Respond

In pairs talk about the following:

Is God calling you to do a certain task from which you are holding back? Do you feel that you are too old to be used? Or too young? Acknowledge that God is in no sense ageist, and then offer yourself again to be used by him.

Affirm the fact that although most of us are 'control freaks', there is a strong biblical mandate to trust and obey.

Pray for one another.

5

The Law and the land

This week's readings...

Exodus 19:1 – 20:21
Exodus 32–34
Joshua 1
Joshua 3,4
Joshua 5:13 – 6:27

Essential 100 pages 41–47

THE BIG STORY

The covenant between man and God moves forward with the giving of the Ten Commandments.

Although Jacob had twelve sons, the resulting twelve tribes of Israel do not include Joseph, but the two half-tribes of his sons Ephraim and Manasseh. Levi's descendants become the priestly tribe and do not inherit a region of the Promised Land.

The covenant God has made with Abraham to give him a land is fulfilled.

Way in

Begin by asking the group to share experiences of people who have been key players in the development of their faith. This might be a Sunday School teacher from childhood years, a minister or friend.

Review

Invite the group members to share what they have written on the 'review' page of *Essential 100*, and to give reactions to what they have read.

Having escaped from Egypt, the people of Israel journeyed through the wilderness and into the Promised Land.

- The Ten Commandments were given by God to Moses on Mount Sinai, not as a set of rules that would take away people's pleasure and freedom, but rather to act as a framework for their relationships with God, each other and material possessions.

- The making and worship of the golden calf revealed the vulnerability of the Israelites' faith.

- Joshua was appointed to succeed Moses.

- Joshua listened to and obeyed God, as he was directed to cross the River Jordan. Setting up the stone memorial would be a reminder of what God had done, for generations to come.

- Joshua once again listened and obeyed the directions God gave him for capturing the city of Jericho.

Going deeper

The Ten Commandments

Take a look at the Ten Commandments (Exodus 20:1–17). What are the implications and challenges for our relationships: with God, with each other and with material possessions.

Which commandments does Jesus build on? How does he take them to a deeper level of application? (See Matthew 5:17–20, 21,22 and 27,28.)

Explore the implications of these developments for us in our Christian living.

Joshua

Joshua is characterised by 'bold faith' and 'humility'. Think about these two characteristics in relation to life and ministry. What might be the benefits and the pitfalls?

Rahab

The account of Rahab is both surprising and challenging. She appears to be a very unsuitable person to be saved, yet her response to the living God means she is kept safe when the walls of Jericho fall.

Can you think of people groups today that could be represented by Rahab? How are they viewed by the Church?

Are there encounters in the life of Jesus that demonstrate a similar learning point?

Respond

In a time of quiet, read slowly through the Ten Commandments, pausing between each one. As you do so together, pray that the Holy Spirit will bring to mind any areas that are especially relevant for you.

What positive qualities do you see in your church leaders? Pray for them now.

Are there any people groups against whom you may have prejudice? Ask God to reveal and remove those barriers. Pray that he will give you a genuine, loving acceptance of them. Is there something you need to do as a result of this? Pray for one another.

6

The judges

This week's readings...

Judges 2:6 – 3:6
Judges 4,5
Judges 6,7
Judges 13–16
Ruth 1–4

Essential 100 pages 48–54

Way in

Think about the four main characters from this week's readings: Deborah, Gideon, Samson, Ruth.

Ask the group to consider which of these they relate to most closely, and why.

Review

Invite the group members to share what they have written on the 'review' page of *Essential 100*, and to give reactions to what they have read.

- The period of the judges is marked by a cycle of disobedience and defeat. The Israelites failed to learn lessons from their own history. Yet, in the midst of the unfaithfulness, some characters stood out from the crowd, pointing people back to God.

- Deborah, the only female judge and an unlikely choice in a male-dominated culture, was obedient to God's call, showing great courage in the face of adversity.

- Gideon, a reticent leader who wanted to be doubly sure that his call really was from God, placed his total trust in God's ability to win the battle, not simply the size of the army.

- Samson, with God-fearing parents who set their son apart from birth, rebelled against the constraints of his parents' religion, resulting in humiliation and captivity.

- Ruth used personal tragedy to develop character and a lasting testimony instead of allowing it to make her bitter and resentful.

Going deeper

Faith in hard situations

Talk about some times when, like Deborah, you have needed faith in the face of a difficult situation.

Discovering God's will

Which is harder: discovering God's will or obeying it? Think about Gideon's guidance experiences, then talk about what methods we might use to know for sure that it is God who is calling us to pursue a certain path?

When loved ones reject God

Remembering Samson, think about Christian families who have experienced their children turning away from God. Explore some of the reasons why this might happen, the resulting feelings of parents and attitudes of others. (Be sensitive and supportive to any in your group for whom this may be an issue.)

Consider some ways in which your church could support families going through the trauma of their children's rebellion against God or church.

If possible, share some stories of how a young person who has turned away from God has later in life come to faith.

Coping with tragedy

Compare the reactions of Naomi and Ruth to what happened to them. How can we help people come through times of personal tragedy in ways that result in the development of strong and positive character and faith? (Although she lived in the period of the judges, Ruth was not a judge.)

Respond

Arrange in advance for group members to bring to this session photos of family and friends with stories that fit into some of the categories you have been thinking about. Place these at the centre of the group. As appropriate, share some of the stories about the people in the photos.

Are you looking for God's guidance? Pray that you will know which way he wants you to go?

How do you view those who have 'gone off the rails'? Pray for Christian families who have children who have turned away from God.

How have you handled tragedy in your life: has it left you bitter and resentful? If so, allow God to break into that area to bring his healing. Or, if you have never had such an experience, pray that should there be such an event, you will be equipped to respond as Ruth did.

Close by praying for one another and for those in the photos whose situations you know.

7

The rise of Israel

THE BIG STORY

The people of Israel want to be like other nations and have a human king. From this follows a succession of kings who rule with varying levels of success.

Honouring God results in prosperity; turning from him leads to all sorts of problems – a pattern seen throughout the rest of Old Testament history.

Way in

David's success in his battle against Goliath is one of the most well known stories in the Bible. Get your group to share examples from their own lives of when they have achieved some great challenge. It could be something physical, practical, to do with a relationship or spiritual.

Review

Invite the group members to share what they have written on the 'review' page of *Essential 100*, and to give reactions to what they have read.

- Hannah cried to God for a son – and was given Samuel.

- The people of Israel wanted to have a king like other nations. Unhappy with having God as their ruler, they demanded a human ruler – and were given Saul.

- Saul failed to be the leader God had looked for, and this resulted in Samuel anointing David as the future king. With David's defeat of Goliath, it wasn't long before Saul was filled with all-consuming jealousy of this gifted young man.

- Despite attempts by Saul to kill him, David responded by sparing Saul's life – just one indication among many that David was walking closely with his God.

▣ Finally, David became king, leading to a period of great success for the Israelite nation.

Going deeper

Waiting on God

What qualities does Hannah display that might be an example for us to follow in situations we are facing at present?

Following the crowd

The people of Israel, God's holy nation, want to be like the surrounding nations and have a human king. As Christians, we are called to have Jesus as our king, yet often we want to be like those around us.

Talk about areas in life that can bring similar conflict for us. How could these lead us to compromise in our holy living for God?

Failure and success

Look again at the sequence of events surrounding the reigns of Saul and David. Where does Saul go wrong? What lies at the heart of David's success? What can we learn from this for our own lives?

Respond

David, although he sometimes fails, seeks God's direction with an open heart; he celebrates all God has done and is doing through his worship, and is focused on God's priorities in his life.

These attitudes give God his rightful place as King. Do these things characterise our lives?

When God works through us, do we have the humility that gives the credit to him, rather than thinking it has been done in our strength?

Think about these things, praying that God would highlight where we are just 'doing things our way', as Saul so often does. Ask that we will instead develop a heart that gives God his rightful place in our lives.

8   The fall of Israel

This week's readings...

2 Samuel 11:1 – 12:25
1 Kings 2,3
1 Kings 8:1 – 9:9
1 Kings 16:29 – 19:18
2 Kings 25

Essential 100 pages 62–68

THE BIG STORY

Disputes about who should rule result in the kingdom of Israel dividing, with Israel in the north and Judah in the south.

Repeated turning from God ultimately means defeat by their enemies, exile and captivity. God, however, does not forget his covenant; there is the promise that 'a remnant will return'.

Way in

We all encounter problems, but one of the greatest antidotes is focusing on the good things God has done for us.

Get the group to share one good thing God has done in their lives. Use these testimonies as a way in to praising God that he is living and active.

Review

Invite the group members to share what they have written on the 'review' page of *Essential 100*, and to give reactions to what they have read.

- King David was so successful yet, despite his openness to God's will, he failed in the events surrounding Bathsheba.

- Solomon sought wisdom, but he, too, had a failing – dabbling in idolatry.

- The dedication of the temple was an amazing event: '…the glory of the LORD filled his temple' (1 Kings 8:11).

- The story moves on to the depths of failure characterised by Ahab and Jezebel. Elijah heads up the remarkable showdown on Mount Carmel – and then flees, feeling rejected and in total despair.

- God had promised not to destroy the world with another flood, but after generations of rebellion against his rule, he used the Babylonians to bring judgement on the city of Jerusalem.

Going deeper

Iron sharpening iron

Others often don't see what is really going on in our lives. So, David, the great, God-following leader, sins. Nathan has a key role in David's repentance.

Proverbs 27:17 says: 'As iron sharpens iron, so one man sharpens another.' How have others helped you to see your failings and consequently to grow in your relationship with God?

Sin and forgiveness

What is the difference between Saul and David, as one is removed but the other is given a second chance? What can we learn from this about repentance, forgiveness and God's grace?

Idols

Solomon's failing is not dealing with idolatry. What things are at risk of becoming idols that we worship in our lives today?

Worship

The dedication of the temple is memorable for one major reason: God turns up in all his glory and fills the place.

How can we make sure that the mechanics of worship in our church don't get in the way of an encounter with the living God?

Victory and despair

We've seen two sides to Elijah's character: victorious on Carmel; in the depths of despair on Horeb. What can we do to develop on-fire faith yet reduce the risk of spiritual and emotional burnout?

Respond

Allow a time of silence for confession of sin. Then, as a sign of God's forgiveness, invite people to write their confessions on pieces of paper, then burn them (with care!).

Reflect for a few minutes on the nature of worship. How can worship become a more meaningful experience?

Pray that the group will develop an open accountability that will enable their faith to grow and their integrity to be maintained.

Encourage everyone to continue engaging with God's Word frequently, as a way of hearing what God wants to say. Pray for each other about this.

9

Psalms and Proverbs

Way in

Get the group to write their own psalm using the following model. Provide each person with a sheet of paper, large enough to be folded eight times. Then:

1 Ask everyone to write across the top of their sheet of paper an opening sentence of praise, eg: 'God, I worship you'.

2 Get everyone to fold back that line of writing, and pass the sheet of paper to the person on their left.

3 On the next line encourage everyone to write an aspect of God's character, starting: 'because you are...' Fold and pass on.

And so on...

4 Another aspect of God's character, starting: 'and...'

5 Two things about how wonderful creation is.

6 Something God does for you, eg 'You guide me'.

7 A message to Jesus, eg 'Jesus, I love you because...'

8 A resolution, eg 'Therefore I will...'

Read your 'psalms' aloud as an opening act of worship.

Review

Invite the group members to share what they have written on the 'review' page of *Essential 100*, and to give reactions to what they have read.

- Psalm 23: David used his own experience as a shepherd to highlight key aspects of God's nature and character.

- Psalm 51: David acknowledged his sinfulness in his relationship with Bathsheba, and sought God's mercy and forgiveness.

- Psalm 103: David praised God for all he is: forgiving, healing, redeeming, renewing, revealing, compassionate, endlessly loving, faithful, ruling.

- The proverbs of Solomon: wise sayings to help us in godly living. Living by them protects us against the consequences of evil, and brings happiness and well-being.
- Solomon highlighted the choices and conflicts that regularly face us: wisdom and folly; humility and pride; God's will and human action.

Going deeper

Repentance

Living in a time when we emphasise the loving and forgiving heart of God means that confession may seem too easy. David affirms that God doesn't want sacrifices of burnt offerings (Psalm 51:16), but how can we ensure that we take sin seriously? How do we respond to sin in our own lives? What does it mean to have 'a broken and contrite heart'?

What could we learn from David's example, referred to in his son Solomon's words in Proverbs 4:3,4, where he writes about the influence of his parents?

Acts 3:19,20 speaks of 'refreshing' being a consequence of repentance. How do these fit together? What do you think is meant by spiritual refreshment?

What is God like?

List all the different qualities of God you can find in Psalm 103. Think of examples from the Bible that demonstrate some of these characteristics of God.

Wisdom

Wisdom and knowledge are very different things: wisdom is demonstrated as we use our knowledge wisely. In 1 Corinthians 1:20, Paul highlights the difference between worldly wisdom and the wisdom of God. Encourage your group to think of some specific examples where this is the case.

Respond

If the group is comfortable to do so, you could place a cross at the centre of the group as a reminder and symbol of God's wisdom. As you focus on this, consider the question below and pray for one another.

Are there areas of your life where you are living according to the wisdom of the world, rather than the wisdom of God? Pray that the Holy Spirit would reorder your thinking, pulling it back into line with God's will.

10   The prophets

This week's readings...

Isaiah 51–53
Jeremiah 1:1 – 3:5
Daniel 6
Jonah 1–4
Malachi 1–4

Essential 100 pages 76–82

THE BIG PICTURE

The prophets are God's spokesmen. Predicting the future is part of what they do, but their main function is to declare God's view of how his people are living in the midst of compromise and waywardness. Warnings, as well as a call to repentance and change, are core to their message.

Way in

Get the group to name as many of the prophets mentioned in the Bible as they can. Explore together what the prophets in the Bible were like, who they were and what role they fulfilled.

Review

Invite the group members to share what they have written on the 'review' page of *Essential 100*, and to give reactions to what they have read.

The five readings in this section look at five of the prophets:

- Isaiah: the heavyweight of the prophets, living during the reigns of several kings. His messages had a clear emphasis on warning and judgement, hope and salvation. God would send a saviour to rescue his people.

- Jeremiah: a young man who was given a frightening message. Yet God took him beyond his human ability, providing the confidence to declare God's warning and his desire to forgive and restore his people.

- Daniel: an exile who was totally committed to living for God no matter what the consequences, knowing that his trust in him would be honoured.

- Jonah: the prophet who tried to run from God. He learned that you cannot hide from God.

■ Malachi: challenged Israel about her unfaithfulness. Judgement is always the consequence of sin.

Going deeper

Called by God

There are many 'ordinary' people in the Bible whom God uses to fulfil his purposes. Think about some examples (eg Jeremiah, Moses, David). What is it about these people that makes them God's choice?

It's easy to think that certain people are called to 'full-time Christian work' while others do 'ordinary' jobs. Can a case be made for this from what the Bible teaches?

If each one of us is called to be a full-time Christian worker wherever God has placed us, what are the implications for how we do our jobs and at the same time fulfil our calling?

What might the implications from this be for how churches equip their members to serve?

Reaching out to non-believers

Most Christians are keen to affirm God's grace, which reaches out to 'sinners' who are out there in the world. But how do you feel about reaching out to those who you might think are undeserving of forgiveness? Or how about people within our church whom we see failing?

To help you in your discussion, look at the parables of 'the lost sheep' and 'the prodigal son' (see Luke 15, also Romans 3:23,24).

Respond

Do you, in fact, have a personal league table of sins, which means that some people don't really 'qualify' for God's love and forgiveness?

Invite God to let his grace sweep through your heart and mind, bringing you again to the point of owning the fact that all have sinned and fall short of God's glory – and that his love embraces anyone who truly repents and he welcomes them into his family.

Have you felt God might be calling you to a specific task, but have shied away owing to feelings of your inadequacy? Ask the group to pray about this for you, that his call would be clarified and that you would have the faith to lay your life completely at his disposal.

11

The living Word

This week's readings...

John 1:1–18
Luke 1
Luke 2:1–40
Luke 3
Matthew 3:13 – 4:17

Essential 100 pages 84–90

Way in

Give each group member a sheet of paper and get them to write down as many names of Jesus as they can think of. Feed back your lists. Encourage each person to share one name that has particular significance for them. Use this as a way into an opening time of worship of Jesus, for who he is and what he has done for us.

Review

Invite the group members to share what they have written on the 'review' page of *Essential 100*, and to give reactions to what they have read.

- Using language from Genesis 1, John began his Gospel by rooting the person of Jesus in the Godhead. Involved from the beginning of time, Jesus was 'God made flesh'.

- Elizabeth and Mary were the people God decided to use as the mothers for John and Jesus. Without fully understanding how this could happen, they committed themselves to God's purposes.

- The greatest miracle of all time, Jesus' birth, took place in a very ordinary context. The first people to meet him were shepherds.

- John the Baptist, the 'greatest prophet' (Luke 7:24–28), proclaimed judgement, hope and – most important – he introduced and prepared the way for Jesus.

- Jesus was baptised and then went into the wilderness where he was tempted by the devil.

Going deeper

God's call and family responsibility

Both Zechariah and Joseph are forced to face up to challenging situations. When a family member is called to a specific task within local church life, this sometimes results in significant pressure on home and family life.

Explore the issues this raises in terms of God's expectations and those of the Church, as well as support towards one's spouse. How do our responsibilities to our families fit with what God has called us to do?

It can be quite difficult to talk about our faith with our families. So can enabling others to enter the spotlight instead of ourselves. Explore what can be learnt from John the Baptist's life in these two areas.

Temptation

Temptation is something everybody experiences. Spend some time exploring the range of things we may be tempted in and by, and the different ways in which temptation comes.

Look at 1 Corinthians 10:12,13. What 'ways out' of temptation are there? Jesus uses the Bible, Paul teaches about the full armour of God (Ephesians 6:10–18). Talk about how both can become effective defences against the attacks of Satan.

Respond

Share together some tempting cakes or chocolates! Then talk about…

Meeting in a small group provides a wonderful opportunity for mutual accountability within a framework of love, trust and acceptance (see Study 8, pages 22 and 23). Does this happen in your group?

Being sensitive to individual feelings and group relationships, explore together whether you are ready to challenge and be challenged by one another? Would you be able to admit to the group that you are being tempted in certain areas?

Are there ways in which you could help one another not to give in to temptation? Would you feel able to confess giving in to temptation to others in the group, knowing you would still be loved and accepted?

Spend some time praying about any temptations you are currently facing. Pray for one another.

12   The teachings of Jesus

This week's readings...

Matthew 5:1 – 6:4
Matthew 6:5 – 7:29
Matthew 13
Luke 10:25–37
Luke 15

Essential 100 pages 91–97

Way in

Divide your group into twos or threes. Ask each group to choose one of the parables that Jesus told and work out a retelling in a modern equivalent context, using a totally different setting and set of circumstances.

Allow each group to present their modern parable.

Review

Invite the group members to share what they have written on the 'review' page of *Essential 100*, and to give reactions to what they have read.

- The Sermon on the Mount: the most well-known of all Jesus' sermons. He defined true happiness, talked about the importance of influencing others and significantly increased the expectations found in the Old Testament for God's people.

- The Lord's Prayer: highlighted two main focal points for prayer – worship and requests.

- The parables of the sower, the weeds, the mustard seed and yeast: all were used to highlight issues surrounding the ongoing battle between Christ and the evil one; the kingdom of God and the powers of darkness.

- The parable of the Good Samaritan: Jesus used this to stress that God doesn't look for men and women with all the right answers, but for those with compassion, resulting in action.

- The parables of the lost sheep, lost coin and lost, or prodigal, son: Jesus had a heart for the lost, wanting to reclaim and restore them, repairing broken lives.

Going deeper

A good sermon

We live in an age that loves entertainment and anecdote. Preachers often feel under pressure to 'perform well' rather than 'preach with power'. What should the role of preaching be? Look together at Jesus' sermon in Matthew 5. With this in mind, formulate a definition of what you think God might class as a good sermon?

Prayer

Our prayers all too often become shopping lists, whereas it is clear that adoration, confession and thanksgiving should also be core elements. Get your group to find psalms that have an emphasis in each of these three areas.

With reference to Matthew 6:6,8,18 and 32, notice how the Father is integrally involved in each of the activities mentioned. How can we develop an 'Our Father' lifestyle, in which all of life becomes prayer?

Loving the lost

The parable of the sower is one of the best known parables of Jesus. Read Matthew 13:1–23 and talk about the implications of the four lots of seed. What steps could your church take to reduce the risk of the first three outcomes?

Look at John 3:16,17, Luke 19:10 and Galatians 6:1,2. Explore how these verses, as well as the parable of the lost, or prodigal, son (Luke 15:11–32), compare with attitudes within church life. How can we demonstrate more clearly God's love for sinners?

(Note: Be sensitive to anyone in your group with a 'prodigal' son or daughter.)

Respond

Think about the parable of the lost son. Where would you place yourself in the parable? The son who has wandered off? The father who is keen to welcome back and restore? The older son, self-righteous and unforgiving? Or another person not mentioned individually in the parable, looking on, slightly detached?

For anyone who has strayed from God, coming back to church is one of the hardest things imaginable, made harder by the reaction from others. Allow the Holy Spirit to challenge you regarding your attitude to 'the prodigals', then pray that your church would be a place full of God's restorative love.

13   The miracles of Jesus

This week's readings...

Luke 9:1–36
Matthew 14:22–36
John 9
Mark 5:1–20
John 11

Essential 100 pages 98–104

Way in

Ask whether anyone in the group has personally experienced or witnessed healing, either supernaturally received, or through God's gift of medicine? Encourage people to share what God did.

Begin the session with a time of prayer, thinking about this session's topic. Pray for wisdom, understanding and sensitivity. Some may have experienced significant pain when a loved one wasn't healed or when God didn't intervene in a miraculous way despite great faith. Pray that, although these things may be outside your own experience, you would nevertheless be open to whatever God wants to say.

Review

Invite the group members to share what they have written on the 'review' page of *Essential 100*, and to give reactions to what they have read.

- Jesus sent out the 12 disciples to cast out demons and heal the sick. This was followed by the feeding of the 5,000, Peter's statement regarding Jesus' true identity and with the transfiguration.

- Jesus walked on the water, and Peter, with an amazing step of faith, got out of the boat to do the same.

- A man blind from birth was healed by Jesus, leading to a very negative response from the religious leaders.

- Jesus cast out demons from a man living in the region of the Gerasenes.

- The death of one of Jesus' friends became the springboard for not just another miracle, but a living parable of what lay ahead in his own life.

Going deeper

Understanding the implications of Jesus' miracles for the life of the Church is a complex and problematic issue that we all have to wrestle with. Be sensitive, starting with an affirmation that there is much that we do not and cannot fully understand.

The miracles of Jesus

Start by getting the group to overview the range of Jesus' miracles, looking at the contexts and the consequences of each. How can you see that the miracles are designed to highlight and emphasise Jesus' verbal teaching? They are not 'stand-alone magic tricks'. As with Peter, allow these truths to lead to a reaffirmation that Jesus is 'The Christ of God'.

Preaching the kingdom

Read Mark 6:6–13. Talk through the experience of the disciples as Jesus delegates responsibility to them to heal the sick, cast out demons and preach the kingdom. How do they feel as they go? What happens?

What do you think will prevent people from seeing and accepting that this is a clear demonstration that God's kingdom is being established on earth?

Talk about ways in which God's power should be demonstrated in our individual lives, and within the life of the Church. See Ephesians 1:18–20, which speaks of the power of God at work within us.

Respond

Jesus often took time out to be alone with his heavenly Father. Spend some time in quietness, inviting God to minister to individual needs, to clarify people's thoughts and to give you a passion to see God move in power within and through the Church.

Close by praying that each group member would know the power of God at work within their life, and would live with the confidence that nothing is impossible for him.

14   The cross of Christ

This week's readings...

Luke 22:1–46
John 18
John 19
John 20,21
Acts 1:1–11

Essential 100 pages 105–111

THE BIG STORY

The death of Jesus becomes the final confirmation and seal of the new covenant God has made with mankind. No longer would regular animal sacrifice be required, Jesus, the perfect sacrifice, has been offered.

Way in

This session's focus on the death of Jesus provides a perfect opportunity to share communion. If this is appropriate within your church's tradition, consider starting or closing in this way.

Encourage group members to build up a mental image of the whipped Jesus – carrying his cross through the city and being nailed to the cross. What are you seeing, thinking and feeling?

Read aloud Isaiah 53:6: '...the Lord has laid on him the iniquity of us all.'

Allow these reflections to lead into a time of confession, followed by worship.

Review

Invite the group members to share what they have written on the 'review' page of *Essential 100*, and to give reactions to what they have read.

- Judas agreed to betray Jesus but, despite knowing this, Jesus still chose to celebrate Passover with him and with Peter, whom Jesus knew would deny him.

- Judas betrayed Jesus with a kiss; Jesus was subsequently arrested. His trial began, without a hint of justice or fairness. Peter denied even knowing Jesus, and the final decision about Jesus' life rested with the Roman governor, Pilate.

- Jesus was sentenced to death, whipped, crucified and then died. Jesus' body was taken from the cross and buried.

- On the Sunday morning, the tomb was found to be empty. The resurrected Jesus appeared: first to Mary, then to the disciples. Jesus shared breakfast with the disciples after a night fishing, followed by the moving account of Peter's reinstatement.

- The final appearance of Jesus to the disciples included the promise of the Holy Spirit, their commission to be his witnesses and then his ascension into heaven.

Going deeper

Denying Jesus

Have you every denied Jesus or, at least, remained silent about your faith? Talk through Peter's circumstances (John 18) and draw out comparisons with situations we might face today.

Read Matthew 10:17–20. How can we prepare ourselves for such times and what might we do when such circumstances occur?

The evidence for the resurrection

It's important that, as Christians, we can talk clearly about the evidence for the resurrection. Talk through these five pointers:

- the disappearance of the body

- the range of people who met the risen Christ

- if there had been no resurrection, the disciples would have known Jesus was a con man

- the transformation of the disciples: fear to confidence

- the rise of the early Church.

Becoming a Christian

The life and death of Jesus make it possible for anyone to become a member of God's family. Think through how you might communicate this clearly and concisely as opportunity arises. Some key verses include: Romans 3:23; Romans 6:23; Ephesians 2:8,9; John 5:24.

Respond

Place a cross at the centre of your group, and encourage everyone to focus on this as you pray together.

Remind one another about the grace of God and his offer of forgiveness and another chance. Pray for each other that there would be such a real experience of God's presence that you will have no doubt that Jesus is alive.

15   The Church is born

This week's readings...

Acts 2
Acts 3:1 – 4:37
Acts 6:8 – 8:8
Acts 8:26–40
Acts 10:1 – 11:18

Essential 100 pages 112–118

THE BIG STORY

God's covenant relationship is now being extended to include people beyond the Jewish nation. Working for the extension of God's kingdom now becomes the responsibility of every member of God's community.

Way in

As a group, 'experience' the events of Acts 2:1–13 together: split the group into 'disciples' and the 'crowd'. Encourage everyone to close their eyes.

Read Acts 2:1: ask the 'disciples', 'What are you feeling at this moment?' Encourage one or two to respond with simple adjectives.

Read verses 2–4, and then ask the same question.

Read verses 5,6, and ask the 'crowd' what they are thinking and feeling.

Now move into a time of open prayer, asking that each group member would have a new encounter with God as his Spirit is present with you in this study.

Review

Invite the group members to share what they have written on the 'review' page of *Essential 100*, and to give reactions to what they have read.

- The day of Pentecost arrived with a dramatic outpouring of the Spirit, resulting in courage for the believers and mass conversions amongst the crowds.

- The disciples were used by God in amazing demonstrations of his power; there was a complete sense of unity and mutual care among the believers.

- Stephen was stoned to death, becoming the first Christian martyr. This was followed by an immediate spread of intense persecution.
- Philip was led by the Holy Spirit onto the desert road to Gaza, where he had the opportunity to explain his faith to an official from Ethiopia.
- Peter had a life-changing vision, through which he came to understand that God now wanted Gentiles as well as Jews to have the opportunity to become members of his holy nation.

Going deeper

The Holy Spirit

Explore the words 'power', 'mission' and 'waiting', thinking about the implications for the Church today.

Sadly, the person of the Holy Spirit is all too often either neglected or misunderstood. The New Testament makes it clear that entering God's family can only happen if the Holy Spirit is involved. Explore together the following passages: John 3:5,6; John 16:7–15; Acts 2:17,18; Ephesians 5:18.

The challenges of living for God

God has never said that being part of his family will mean all our problems and struggles disappear. What can we learn from the death of Stephen? Are there implications for people in other parts of the world facing severe persecution? What are the challenges for ourselves?

Guidance

How does God 'nudge' people today to do something, or go somewhere, like Philip? How can we be sure that something is godly direction, not just 'my idea'?

One in Christ

The New Testament makes it clear that, through the death of Jesus, barriers that divided people into subgroups have all been removed. How does this challenge and transform the attitude of the Church, as it thinks about what it means to be inclusive?

Respond

Talk about how you share your faith with others. Do you seize opportunities or back away from them? Do you rely on your own eloquence, or on the Holy Spirit to empower you?

Allow a time of quiet – for God to speak, direct and challenge. 'Be filled with the Spirit' (Ephesians 5:18) is not simply an event, but should be an ongoing experience. Encourage each person to consider whether they desire to have a deeper experience of God's Spirit. If so, pray for that now.

16   The travels of Paul

This week's readings...

Acts 9:1–31
Acts 13,14
Acts 15
Acts 16–20
Acts 25–28

Essential 100 pages 119–125

Way in

Give the opportunity for group members to share how they made a decision to follow Christ. Use these stories to lead into a time of praise to God for the fact that he calls people into his family, and for the way he relates to each person as an individual.

Review

Invite the group members to share what they have written on the 'review' page of *Essential 100*, and to give reactions to what they have read.

- Saul, the angry antagonist of Jesus' followers, had an encounter with Jesus, was called by God and then became a wholehearted follower of Jesus.

- Paul and Barnabas journeyed together to share the Good News. Showing remarkable courage, their sole intention was to see others become members of God's family.

- There was conflict within the early Church as to who 'qualified' to be classed as a true believer. The believers met together to discuss this.

- Paul remained totally focused on God's call. He waited on God for direction, he sometimes seemed to have gone the wrong way, but even when he went the right way his life was far from problem free!

- Back in Jerusalem, Paul was arrested and put on trial. This was not the end for Paul's ministry. Rather, it enabled him to preach the Good News to significant political figures and to take the gospel further afield.

Going deeper

New believers

Read 1 Corinthians 9:19–23. What does this say to us regarding the ways we seek to reach out into our neighbourhoods with the Good News of

Jesus? What safeguards are needed to make sure that identification with society doesn't lead to conforming with it, and a subsequent compromise of faith?

Read Acts 15:1–21. What is our attitude towards new believers? How are they received in your church, particularly when elements of their 'old life' might still be being worked through? Are there pressures to conform to church expectations of behaviour, dress or language and, if so, are they appropriate?

Some churches seem to behave as if you need to be an experienced Christian before you can be used by God. For Paul, his call to serve seems to be one with his conversion. Do you think that the New Testament suggests the need for a 'probationary period' or should we think in terms of every believer having a mission, a purpose, a call?

Recognising God's call

How can we help each other determine what that call is, and then continue to live with a real sense of vision and purpose?

How should we respond when people make mistakes and try to go down a wrong path (Acts 16:7)?

Sometimes we assume we know God's way because everything falls into place easily; at other times we might decide something isn't God's will because there are so many difficulties. Compare these viewpoints with the situations Paul faces while he is travelling the path God has chosen for him.

Respond

Help people focus on the idea of mission by placing a globe or world atlas at the centre of your group. Where are you involved in mission? Through actions? Through prayer?

In a time of quietness, ask God to show you what purposes he has for your life. Are you wandering fairly aimlessly? Or do you know the specific mission God has called you to, within life, within the local church?

Support and help one another in thinking this through and praying for God's will to be revealed.

17 Paul to the churches

This week's readings...

Romans 8
Galatians 5:16 – 6:10
Ephesians 6:10–20
Philippians 4:2–9
Colossians 1:1–23

Essential 100 pages 126–132

Way in

Working as a group, create a prayer using some of the phrases Paul used in his prayers for the believers in the letters in this week's readings.

Then split into pairs and simply pray for each other using this prayer and incorporating your partner's name.

Here are some references you could use: Ephesians 1:15–23; Ephesians 3:14–21; Philippians 1:3–11; Colossians 1:9–12; 1 Thessalonians 3:13; 1 Thessalonians 5:23; 2 Thessalonians 1:11,12; 2 Thessalonians 2:16,17; 2 Thessalonians 3:5,16.

Review

Invite the group members to share what they have written on the 'review' page of *Essential 100*, and to give reactions to what they have read.

Each of this week's readings have taken extracts from some of Paul's letters.

- Romans 8: Paul began with the basics of the gospel, then moved on to the tension between having our lives controlled by our sinful nature or the Holy Spirit. The chapter concludes with an affirmation of the overall victory for those in God's family.

- Galatians 5 and 6: Paul contrasted the actions flowing from our sinful nature with the life the Holy Spirit is seeking to grow in us.

- Ephesians 6: Paul made it clear there is a battle going on between God and Satan. In order to stand firm, we need to be proactive in staying strong, standing our ground, standing firm, being alert and praying in the Spirit.

- Philippians 4: Paul discovered we can know God's peace no matter what circumstance we find ourselves in.

- Colossians 1: There was a serious risk that believers at Colosse were being drawn away from the true teachings of their new found faith. Paul addressed the matter by affirming their enthusiasm when they first

received the Good News of Jesus, and then restating the central elements
of the gospel message.

Going deeper

Everything works for good

Romans 8:28 is an important verse, yet easily misrepresented. There are
two popular interpretations:

1 Despite problems and difficulties occurring in our lives, God can use our
situation and bring good out of it.

2 Everything that happens in our lives is planned by God, so good will
come from it.

Talk about these two viewpoints. What do you think Paul actually meant?

Living by the Spirit

There are two ways we can be helped to walk the path God wants for us:
help from one another; help from the Holy Spirit. How can both of these
work in practice? (See also Proverbs 27:17; Galatians 6:1,2.)

Talk about what it means to 'live by the Spirit', be 'led by the Spirit' and
'keep in step with the Spirit' (Galatians 5:16,18,25).

Put on the armour of God

No one is safe (1 Corinthians 10:12; 1 Peter 5:8)! What do you think it
means in practice to 'put on the full armour of God' (Ephesians 6:10,11)?

Respond

Think about your life at this time. Are you facing pressures, temptations,
compromises of faith or lifestyle?

Depending on how well group members know each other, encourage them
to share in pairs the areas mentioned above.

Read 1 Corinthians 10:13 aloud to the group followed by Romans 8:37–39.

Encourage your group to think about the fruit of the Spirit (Galatians
5:22,23). Are there any with which you particularly struggle? Agree to focus
on these every day over the next week.

18

Paul to the leaders

This week's readings...

1 Timothy 3
1 Timothy 6:3–21
2 Timothy 2
2 Timothy 3:10 – 4:5
1 Thessalonians 4:13 – 5:11

Essential 100 pages 133–139

Way in

Start by trying to create as comprehensive a list of gifts from the New Testament as you can think of (no looking to begin with!). Then add other skills or talents to your list.

Encourage each person to write their own name at the bottom of a sheet of A4 paper. Then, everyone should pass their paper to their neighbour, who should write a gift that they feel the person has, at the top of the sheet, fold it back and then pass it on to the next person round. Keep doing this until each person in the group receives their sheet of paper back again.

Review

Invite the group members to share what they have written on the 'review' page of *Essential 100*, and to give reactions to what they have read.

- Paul outlined the high standards to be expected from Church leaders.

- Money is not evil in itself, but it must be kept in its appropriate place.

- Paul was Timothy's mentor, and used parallels with a soldier, athlete, farmer and workman to highlight the importance of staying focused on the task he was called to fulfil.

- Paul concluded his writings to Timothy with three final thoughts: suffering is inevitable for Christians; all scripture is useful; we must follow God's call wholeheartedly.

- Paul wanted his readers to understand that the return of Jesus would definitely take place, but no one knew when.

Going deeper

Gifts from God

Some Christians live as if God intends only a select few people to have roles within the life of the local church. Look at these key points from 1 Corinthians 12:

- There are many different gifts. (vs 4,5)
- God decides who has which. (v 11)
- All are given for the benefit of the Church. (v 7)
- There is no place for pride or inferiority. (vs 21–25)

Going back to your list of gifts in *Way in*, talk about the range of gifts in the New Testament (read Romans 12:6–8 alongside 1 Corinthians 12).

Read the parable of the talents (Matthew 25:14–30) and talk through the implications this raises for individuals and the local church.

Money

What is God's attitude towards us accumulating money? (See Luke 12: 16–21)

What should our attitude be towards money? (See 1 Timothy 6:6–10)

What does the Bible teach about giving money? (See 1 Corinthians 16:2; 2 Corinthians 9:7)

The Bible

God has given us the Bible as a source of information, but also as a means of transformation. What are the practical implications of 2 Timothy 3:16,17, and also Hebrews 5:11 – 6:3.

What could be the impact for church life if the local church is made up of people who are immature in their faith?

Mentoring

Paul is Timothy's mentor. What are the benefits of mentoring? Are there ways this could be established within your church, perhaps with new Christians or between old and young people?

Respond

What gifts has God given you? What gifts has God given to others in your group? How does he want them used in the life of the Church?

Are you taking seriously God's expectations regarding the use of your money? Is there an action you need to take?

Is there someone God has placed on your heart whom he wants you to come alongside? Pray quietly that God would confirm this and show you how to move forward with the idea.

19   The apostles' teaching

This week's readings...

1 Corinthians 13
2 Corinthians 4:1 – 6:2
1 Peter 1:1 – 2:12
James 1,2
1 John 3:11 – 4:21

Essential 100 pages 140–146

Way in

Paul was a great thinker, Peter a strong fighter, James a doer and John had a deep concern for love. Ask your group which of these four characteristics they most closely associate themselves with, and then share answers.

Review

Invite the group members to share what they have written on the 'review' page of *Essential 100*, and to give reactions to what they have read.

▪ This week's readings began with Paul's well-known poem of love (1 Corinthians 13). It answered the question, 'What is love?' and then went on to outline how following such a path is the best way to live.

▪ In 2 Corinthians, Paul highlighted our status as new creations flowing from our reconciliation with God, and the subsequent responsibility we have to share this Good News with those around us.

▪ Peter's confidence came from his encounter with the risen Christ. He was sure about the promise of new birth, our living hope and being with Jesus for eternity. Heaven is the believers' true home; in this world we are like aliens in a foreign land.

▪ James was a doer and described some of the practicalities of faith. He made it clear that persecution should be seen as opportunity for growth. He spoke about controlling the tongue. Perhaps his most well known challenge is that faith without works is dead (James 2:17).

▪ John drew out three essential aspects of true faith: belief in Jesus, receiving the Holy Spirit and loving others sacrificially.

Going deeper

Reconciliation

Read Galatians 3:26–28. There are three elements of reconciliation made possible by the cross in these verses: between man and God; between people groups that would humanly speaking be at odds; amongst God's people.

What might the implications of these be for your church?

Talk about the sorts of tensions and divisions that can occur within the Church. How can we demonstrate a commitment to living as people of reconciliation?

How should differences and relationship breakdowns be handled among believers? Look at Matthew 6:14,15, Matthew 18:15–17, Colossians 3:13 and 1 Peter 4:8 for some more help with this.

Faith and 'works'

'Faith without deeds is dead' (James 2:26). Explore how we can live in ways that will demonstrate our faith. Matthew 25:31–46 and Acts 4:32–35 could help you further with this.

Heaven

Peter affirms with confidence an eternal happy ending (1 Peter 1:4). What are the main aspects of our eternal inheritance? Find these key concepts: prepared by God; eternal; no sin, suffering or sadness; dwelling in God's presence; worship.

How do you feel when you think of heaven? How does it affect the way you worship and the way you live now? Look at 1 Peter 2:11,12.

Respond

James speaks of the importance of listening to God through his Word, and then acting on it. Picking up on the issues of living as people of reconciliation, spend some time asking God if there is anyone you need to be reconciled with. Allow the Holy Spirit to highlight any relationship that needs sorting, and then pray for the grace and opportunity to do so.

Close by praising God that our reconciliation with him, made possible through the cross, means we can look forward to eternity in his presence.

20

This week's readings...

Revelation 1
Revelation 2:1 – 3:22
Revelation 4:1 – 7:17
Revelation 19,20
Revelation 21,22

Essential 100 pages 147–153

THE BIG STORY

God's covenant will be finally completed with God's people living with him in the new heaven and new earth for eternity.

Way in

In this last study based on the E100 programme, share the things that have particularly stood out, surprised or enlightened you during your journey through the Bible.

Spend time thanking God for his Word, for the many insights revealing who he is and for the way that he has shown us his plan of salvation through its pages.

Review

Invite the group members to share what they have written on the 'review' page of *Essential 100*, and to give reactions to what they have read.

- John received a new revelation of Jesus. He has come as Saviour in the past: in the future he will come as Judge.
- The seven messages to the churches reveal the depth of care Jesus has for his Church. He encourages them but also challenges.
- John had a vision of heaven and, although the events that he describes are complex, the end result will be overwhelming as people of all nations worship Jesus, the Lamb of God.
- John saw the end of the world like a joyful wedding celebration, with Jesus and the Church as groom and bride. Satan's destruction and the defeat of evil is guaranteed, so, too, the fact that believers will be saved.
- John's vision depicted the overwhelming beauty of our eternal dwelling place. Everything will be new and God will dwell with his people forever.

Going deeper

Walking with God

Revelation 1. Look out for these five aspects of John's experience: he worships; he is obedient to God's Word; he focuses on Jesus; he embraces the Holy Spirit; he endures suffering.

This is a great example for developing our walk with God. Explore how each can be developed in and become part of our daily lives.

Letters to the churches

Smyrna and Philadelphia, both poor and weak, receive words of commendation, but no criticism. What are some implications of this for the Church today, where often success and power are seen as important?

What might be in a letter to your church?

Judgement

There are many misconceptions about judgement. Explore this topic with the help of some of the Bible passages below. (All who have accepted Jesus as their Saviour and Lord are guaranteed a place in heaven for eternity.)

When will judgement happen? (Mark 13:32–37; John 5:28,29; 1 Corinthians 15:51–53; 1 Thessalonians 4:13–17)

Who will be judged? (Matthew 16:27; Matthew 25:31–33; 2 Corinthians 5:10)

For what will people be judged? (Matthew 7:21–23; Matthew 12:36,37; Matthew 25:14–30; Matthew 25:31–46; Revelation 20:12)

Heaven

Share together what you are particularly looking forward to in heaven.

Respond

In advance, prepare a large, simple drawing of a church. When everyone has arrived, write each name somewhere on the drawing. Cut it into pieces with one name on each piece.

Give everyone a piece of the 'puzzle' and together quickly make it, with names showing.

Now, take some time to consider how you fit into the picture of the church. Are you hot, cold or lukewarm? Alive or dead? Hard working for the kingdom, or have you forsaken your first love? Faithful or compromising? Persevering or easily led astray? Be open to God challenging you, and then respond as appropriate for you.

Praise Jesus for the victory he has won for us! Worship God for all he has planned for his people in the future.